The abilities in me

Foundation

www.theabilitiesinme.com
Registered Charity No: 1197965

ARFID, also known as Avoidant/Restrictive Food Intake Disorder is a condition characterised by a person having a very limited diet, not due to body image concerns like in anorexia or bulimia, but because of a lack of interest in eating; avoidance based on the sensory characteristics of food, such as texture, smell, taste, or appearance; or fear of aversive consequences, like choking or vomiting. The key is to make this information understandable and relatable to children, emphasising empathy, understanding, and supportive behaviours.

"This book is to provide awareness for the children growing up with ARFID, also known as Avoidant/Restrictive Food Intake Disorder

Published by Inclusive Tales Publishing in association with Bear With Us Productions

© Inclusive Tales Publishing
The Abilities In Me - Arfid

ISBN Paperback: 9798322220220
ISBN Hardcover: 9781068608230

Written by Gemma Keir
Illustrated by Yevheniia Lisovaya
Edited by Emma Lusty and Claire Bunyan

www.theabilitiesinme.com
www.justbearwithus.com

The abilities in me

in me

Arfid

Written by Gemma Keir

Illustrated by Yevheniia Lisovaya

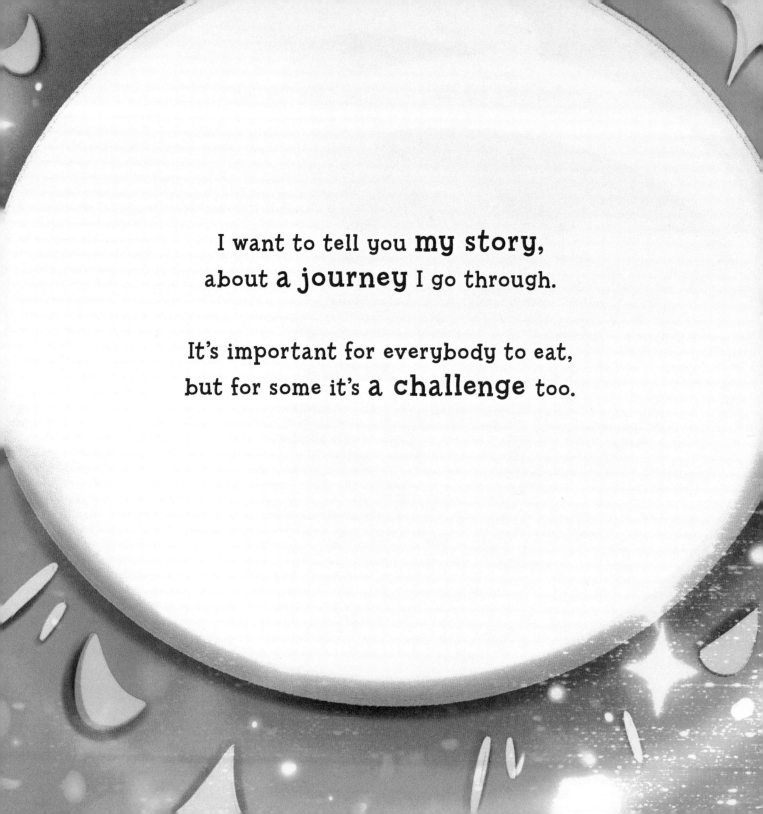

I want to tell you **my story**,
about **a journey** I go through.

It's important for everybody to eat,
but for some it's **a challenge** too.

Some children **love to eat** all foods
and they like to try new things.

But **for others food can be hard to eat**
and scary thoughts it can bring.

I have a condition called **ARFID**.
It affects the way I am with food.

It's short for **Avoidant/Restrictive Food Intake Disorder**
and it can really affect my mood.

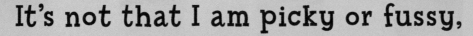

It's not that I am picky or fussy,
I just really can't decide.
I like to make sure my food is **chopped up**
and that it's been
cooked on the inside.

Some children like to separate food,
so it's not together on their plate.
Tasting textures one by one,
can still make meals taste great!

ARFID can leave you feeling worried
about how food looks, smells or tastes.
I also worry about the texture,
whether it's soft, hard, rubbery, wet or paste.

creamy

paste

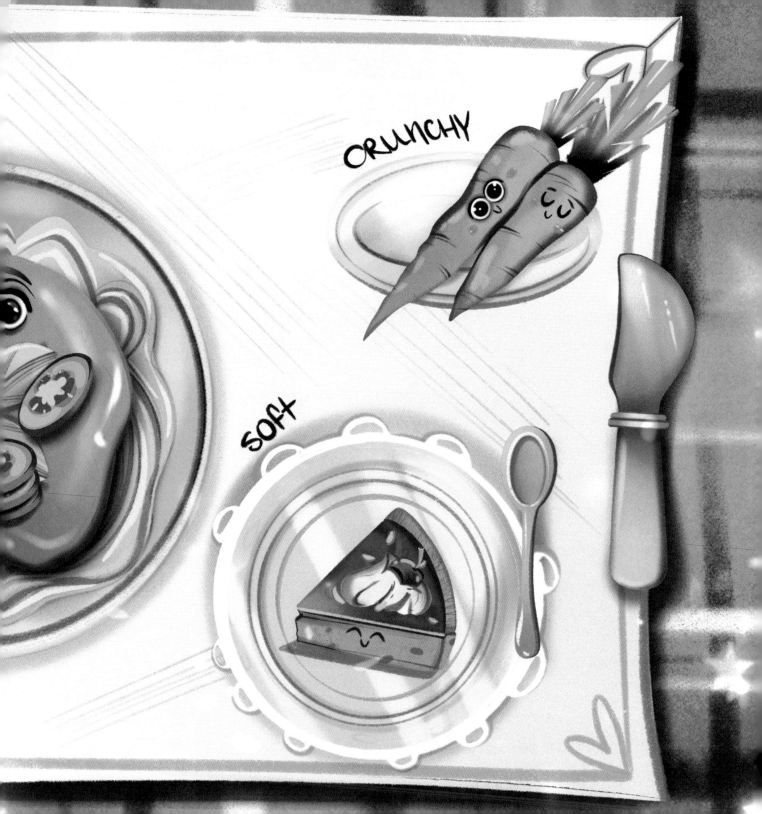

It's not about **how you want to look.**
It's about **how food makes you feel.**

It could be related to senses, or a phobia,
or feeling scared of choking on a meal.

Sometimes I can feel alone and different,
because I don't think anyone understands.
It's hard to explain when you feel a certain way,
but there are people there to hold my hand.

I like to talk to **my therapist,**
about how **I face my fears.**
It's nice to have someone who **listens,**
supports me and wipes away my tears.

Some children like to eat the same things,
it's what they know and it feels safe.

Like the texture of chicken nuggets stays the same,
whereas fruit can be squishy like grapes.

Having **friends** who understand,
can make a big difference to me.
Just because I have my struggles,
I still have so many abilities!

I love to visit the **theme park**,
and go on all the rides.
Even though I have ARFID,
I still like new things to try

Over time I have tried different foods
which takes a lot of bravery.
But sometimes I like to keep to my favourites,
as it is much more comfortable for me.

When I am surrounded by my family
and dinner time is about to arrive,
I like to look at my food plan ahead,
so I don't get a sudden surprise.

Just know that you are not alone,
don't feel afraid to say it's too much.
If you're feeling anxious and worried,
remember...

You've got this! You're enough!

Step by step, you'll find your way
and you may try something new.
Just remember that you are amazing
and people care about you!

So now you know about ARFID
and the journey I go through.
Let's be friends and you can tell me,
What abilities are in you?

The Abilities in Me Foundation aims to raise awareness of special educational needs and conditions that children may encounter. We have an ever-growing book series written for young people that celebrates what these children can do, rather than what they cannot do. The Foundation also provides community support through forums and special events and works with schools to deliver educational workshops.

At the Abilities in Me, we want all children, regardless of their barriers to feel accepted and understood. The books are inspired by real children and experiences and they enable parents and teachers to talk about different needs and conditions with their children in a fun, safe and engaging way.

Our book series has had such a positive impact on children around the world and we will continue to widen our range and encourage further research and funding into different conditions. The Abilities in Me Foundation aims to raise funds to support worthy causes and by bringing awareness into schools, we hope that this will encourage kindness and reduce bullying.

Registered Charity No: 1197965

Find out more information via our website **www.theabilitiesinme.com**
 @theabilitiesinmebookseries

Check out our bookshelf!

    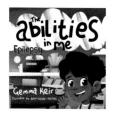

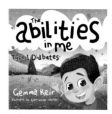   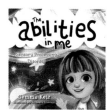 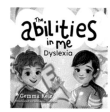

available at
amazon

Made in the USA
Coppell, TX
25 March 2025

47535290R00019